The Empty Grandstand

Lloyd Jones

Lloyd Jones is one of New Zealand's most innovative and accomplished writers. A former journalist who has travelled the world and lived for extended periods in other countries, he has published award-winning short stories, novellas, novels, essays, and a memoir. His novels include *The Book of Fame*, winner of the Tasmania Pacific Prize for Fiction; *Mister Pip*, winner of the Commonwealth Prize for Literature and shortlisted for the Man Booker Prize, *Hand Me Down World*, shortlisted for the Berlin International Prize for Literature, *The Cage*, and *The Fish*. He is a New Zealand Arts laureate and recipient of the Prime Minister's Prize for Literature. *The Empty Grandstand* is his first book of poems.

Lloyd Jones

The Empty Grandstand

UPSWELL

First published in Australia in 2024
by Upswell Publishing
Perth, Western Australia
upswellpublishing.com

Upswell operates in the city of Perth, on ancient country of the Whadjuk
people of the Noongar nation who remain the spiritual and cultural
custodians of this beautiful land. We acknowledge their continuing
connection to country and express gratitude to elders past and present for
their strength and creativity…Always was, always will be, Aboriginal land.

ISBN: 978-0-645-98401-9

A catalogue record for this
book is available from the
National Library of Australia

Cover design by Chil3, Fremantle
Typeset in Foundry Origin by Lasertype

Euan Macleod is a painter, born in Christchurch in 1956. He moved
to Sydney in 1981 where he continues to live and work.

for Carrie

Contents

Music lessons 11

approximately 12

in the crowd 13

Opening of the new grandstand 15

the histories 20

Sailing lessons 21

Portrait of a sailing ship 23

Study of my older brother 24

Young Herodotus 25

Herodotus's certification 26

Your eyes   your eyes 27

Smells of the old grandstand 28

Low tide 29

In my father's country 30

Ode to the mothers 31

I'm waving to can't see me anymore 33

Trapeze artists 34

There is the telephone box bright red like a woman's shoe 35

in America   36

Mistaken identity   37

*'They know they are white, but they must
not know what they know.'*   39

Cofferdam   40

What will you admit about yourself?   41

Vanity   42

Borderlands   43

In free fall   44

Local Beauties   45

5 Studies of my father   46

Traffic   47

Museum   48

We were sailing confidently   49

Log   50

Abandoned city   51

Misplaced things   52

Scruples   53

The decommissioning of the old grandstand   54

Junior geography   56

High Anxiety   57

Non-organic rubbish collection   58

Bonfire   59

At the change of tide   60

The new neighbourhood   63

Interview with great granddaughter from
the future   64

My room at White's   68

Look at the dotterels   71

Log   72

Log   73

Log   75

It has been announced   76

The wishing well   77

There's a war on. There is always a war on.   78

Resumption of interview with great
granddaughter from the future   80

Memory is in the room next door   82

Log   85

Tourist   86

The threat at mid-tide   87

Log   89

The birds of Whakanewha   91

Accept without judgement their fossick
through broken homes   93

In the world of silhouettes   94

New coordinates   95

Log   96

The night desk   97

Blackbird   99

compass   100

Dawn   101

To bring to   103

The news of the day   104

Neighbourhood watch   107

Herodotus in winter   108

Whakanewha   110

in sleep I return to the grove of the forest   111

Across the harbour in April   112

acknowledgements   113

Music lessons

We are given ukuleles to cradle.

Some of us pluck a string – some of us smash

ukuleles on the ground to make a sound.

Some of us use the ukuleles to bash

one another over the head.

The instruments are taken away &

we are each given a certificate.

Our names are very prominent.

approximately

A tree's new

spring

growth

shakes lightly

near a man

sawing wood.

Are we in the right place?

Is it here?

Are we there?

On the platform we turn to & away

from one another.

in the crowd

A smell of coats, dry sweat, stale perfume, apple, smoke, diesel fumes

from the hot dog truck, cold salty air, mandarin, alcohol, its breathy

perch, a circulating air of ruin & old lies, smells of the unwashed,

other smells made vital by their absence, hay, horse shit, spilt milk,

coal dust, leather, musk, pressed flowers, starch, & healing salts,

soaps made of tallow, ink from bark, make-shift poultices, wounds

weeping through bandages, the pleasing smell of damp dog skin, pipe

smoke, chicory...cold mutton, plasticine, cigars. Grey men break

away to find a place to piss, their eyes turned from our casual glance,

their faces pulled by empty thought. A mother sets her toddler down,

squats him over a gutter, then wipes him clean with a fistful of

napkins from the hot dog vendor. An elegant woman brushes a strand

of silver hair away from her eye. She's been watched her entire life.

Now, aged, and slow, she walks with see-sawing shoulders, as though

holding shopping bags. Our mouths twist, like beasts with trapped

desire too large to get at a flower. And through our man-made tunnels

drive ourselves out of the crowd. Our animal scent on us. Brown

faces with lidded eyes. Black and grey top knots. Bone combs. Walnut

wrinkles. Dressed in dog skin and cloaks of bird feathers. Some with

teeth yellowed from fever and war. Bloodshot eyes, hands balled to

fists, bristly, angry...filed teeth. Trusted by ants at last. We carry

them in our trouser cuffs. We welcome all onto our moving limbs, bacteria, small birds, the smaller ones tucked up inside of themselves like they are riding coach. Everyone bright and enthusiastic as if bringing a donation to a charity event.

Slap. Slap. We walk on, trophies shining in our eyes. As though our slapping feet have acquired divinity.

Opening of the new grandstand

Our seats are up 'in the gods' Row Y.

Look how high we are   Look!

Some of the younger kids cover their eyes,

some are crying.

Down past our toes our lives fall sharply away.

We sit my father & me   with other boys & their dads & some

fathers without boys.

We peep down over our knees at the tiny rectangle of green far below.

A boy in row W refuses to & when he covers his eyes with his hands

the coward is put against a wall & shot & my father says *look, he was*

given a fair go & all the other fathers nod &

my head is cloud bombed by *fair goes.*

When I start to tip

I press down through my feet to glue me in place.

My father asks why I am clutching the seat.

In case I fly away.

Icicles break & fall away from his face as he smiles.

Then the gale does a crazy turn around the upper stand lifting hats off

our fathers' heads, & I worry   I worry the stand will keel over.

 Some of the smaller kids are brave enough to bawl.

A woman in a white coat – she must be the nurse - shepherds a line of

terrified kids down the steep concrete steps.

I wave to get the nurse's attention. My father slaps my hand down,

then after a quick look over his shoulder slaps me with the rolled-up

programme.

Nah, he says, like he was just joking & now it's a joke he slaps me

with it again.

I know he won't leave. Our seats are free because he is one of the

welders who stood on steel beams & worked behind a shower of

sparks to make the grandstand stick together.

This is his due & now we must suffer & fall with him.

At breakfast I saw him crack two eggs & overlook the pieces of broken

shell in the mix.

Now I worry about loose bolts.

We are walloped by a fresh gust – the stand shakes &

we turn into one huge, slapped face.

A boy selling meat pies is stretchered down to Casualty.

We get up to swap seats & my father does that fatherly thing of

spreading his arms to prevent me falling.

I sit down & he sticks his cigarette in my mouth to free up his hands

to fasten the hood of my parka.

the crowd roars

        to the edge of our seats we move,

        now onto our feet

& we cheer & cheer

at the backs of the coats & shaven necks

God how I cheer

for an event I cannot see

but discover on the arranged pleasure of

my father's face

he too was part & played.

II

We perch in something

broken & fragile

A web perhaps

A shattering loosely held

A city of air

for a bird to fly in & out of

godless

like a crumpled acropolis

shouldering a sun-lit past &

hearsay

The complaint of Banks, for example

Unable to hear

himself think

for dawn

chorusing in a

now-dead forest

 a made up

place to make up

ourselves

shouting our *Tarzan* nonsense

like all secrets

eventually we

discover

museum drawers of

stuffed birds stitched up

with closed eyes

each in a bed of cotton wool.

III

Of the leftover traces... shed skin,

jewellery, various

  rejectmenta, breath over the shaving mirror, grubby

finger marks, hair in the plughole. Fingertips

pressed into a toilet roll, a reminder

of Crusoe's discovery of

another's footprint in the sand.

the histories

The first pā encountered is the one in the class for halfwits   built

out of matchsticks   I look at it

with a prior knowledge of a knowledge I do not have &

wait for the teacher to say no that is not right or accidentally is

without it being totally right - for which the phrase *if you see what I*

mean was originally invented –

then the bell rings & we run outside to

chase girls across the playing field in a make-believe

game we feverishly believe in.

Sailing lessons

We are put into boats. Class Optimist.

Knobbly knees of the larger children point up. They look like they are

sitting inside a cardboard box.

We learn to duck under the swinging boom – how we love the halfwit

word *boom* – and the instant fill of air in sail.

A man wading in the sea yells into a megaphone – *Tack! Tack!*

We absorb wind shifts & learn to leverage off surprise, after surprise.

The days roll on forever.

White is still just a colour, seagull shit,

quick to vanish behind Persil, bedsheets, and sail,

aspirin and women playing croquet and bread rolls,

and a particular kind of sea yarny novel:

White angels at dawn & the crew rub their eyes at the sight

of the frozen figures in the rigging. One man's upper and lower

jaw connected by frozen strands of spittle...eyelids half closed &

frozen before they could properly close... hands iced to the masts to

be chipped off & first a hand freed & an arm drops then the ice cracks

around the other hand & the man cartwheels into the sea. Around noon

clean air blows in from warmer parts. Across the decks a cry to

put up the sails & below decks the captain dips his pen and enters

for '5th of May Good Hope five men lost to natural causes.'

The sixth, who survived the night in the rigging, authored the novel.

Portrait of a sailing ship

It looks almost real.

The artist must have looked

as he drew –

but not at the sea.

The tossing waves – a confusion

of the artist's mind, froth

and rollers, pure imagination.

Study of my older brother

One foot on a kitchen chair, a telescope in his hand.

As he describes the world outside, one of the kitchen lights explodes &

I go on banging my spoon on the highchair.

Some of his stories are not quite legal & when some of the sentences end

in police sirens   mum dives under the table &

dad sets aside his knife & fork.

Young Herodotus

We ride our dogs out to the street.

We sit like proud little emperors.

We pat the moist noses & their soft eyes do not blink.

We ride our dogs by ransacked houses &

our dogs on heavy haunches step easily.

They raise a leg & sniff each other.

We pick out a distant shining house window &

in that direction our mounts go on padded paws.

Neighbours peer out from the edges of curtains.

We hold up a hand to let them know they are safe.

We ride our dogs in the exotic fumes

from a passing rubbish truck.

We ride on in hope those who knew us as babies

will see us differently now.

Herodotus's certification

I am *called upon as witness.*

Is that an elephant?

It is not a serious question – it is to find out

if I am alert to other possibilities.

Is that hair?

Is that bone?

Is that blood?

The questions melt away to the dead fact

of a dead dog on the road.

Likewise, the stinky smoke pouring from a brick chimney &

blood seeping out its brick door.

The butcher's knives shine fondly.

The hills are conveniently asleep.

How happy everything looks to be   exactly

as it is.

Your eyes   your eyes

CDE

has become

CDE

Now in a dark room the letters that will solve the confusion -

LOPT

You squint   after the tiny letters on the horizon -

Lgpi

A stigmata or occlusion obstructs the view.

Glasses are recommended to restore cows to a field.

Smells of the old grandstand

Grass, red orgasmic light, animal liver

Old programmes, their pages pressed together, despair at what might
have been

Concrete steps, a cold smell of economy

A stench of corpse on the wind from the 'works'

Confusions arising from green grass & meat production & the day's
'excellent playing conditions'

Sweet body odour, steady cigarette smoke, a rostered-on contentment

Oilskin, safe practicality

Damp wool

Damp socks

Wet leather

An odour of anxiety having run its course in sodden cardboard
tickets of admission

A cold pie & surprise at the size of a muddy hoof print

Shouted air

Obsolete air, like the open mouth of a corpse after the violence has
passed

Low tide

I sweep the beach for the past / not a big past / but a century's loose
change /
A button off a tunic of a World War One soldier / a blistered cannon
ball / old currency

In my father's country

I think of a dry dock, a ship

perched

like a model of a ship without a sea, above

an abyss, where a night

tosses against itself.

In my father's country words

lead nowhere.

In my father's country

a man on a bronze horse waits

for an abandoned century

 to catch him up.

In my father's country

no one is at home,

to fix a lopsided picture.

Ode to the mothers

Shelled peas, cigarette smoke
silent faces grieve

daughters our age. To show how much
we want to hold them, we hurl beer bottles

at the boarded entrance. After we smash the beer
bottles, we throw rocks. The daughters shrug,

unfold their arms.
Some turn round for home.

Up in Row Y, with a mother's daughter
we sit in our own scoop of air,

our broken tongues
set at the edge of a grassy plain,

our warm hug, classically defined, like
the spoils of the Trojan War.

A windswept dreariness, brown

turning leaves,

far below, kids shout at a dog

to jump through a hoop they've set on fire.

What were we so desperate to see?

I'm waving to can't see me anymore

dawn / she / as I knew her then / faded now –

to drone of a plane summoned to an off-ramp / in the sky –

a ferocious squawk / and the gulls are sucked into -

the jet stream of a headline / extinction / dawn –

such beauty slides by

Trapeze artists

rusted rooves / huddled shadows / small town grievance / it is too
hot / there is too much rain / too much frost / battered hills / where
sheep trickle / like granules of salt

for practice we leap out of trees / our sniggering
little ape faces / flattened by the rushing air / without a thought
to landing / it is the air we are after / its sweet release

There is the telephone box bright red like a woman's shoe

Sunstruck / at the edge of the sea

There

you are / ankle-deep in sand / calling your mother / to say / that night

you will be on a flight to LA

You do not hear her say of over there –

                  all the birds are dead

 You do not

                        hear

You put her on hold &

drop down to do up a shoelace.

in America

Everywhere   dead birds

            curled up, like leaves.

It is the fall   the great fall.

So sometimes they are people

            sleeping in the wild

A barefoot woman runs by with battery acid in her veins   weeping

battery acid she pleads

            for help   from God

then anyone, anyone at all & *I bury my eyes in a cough & crouch*

down to tie a shoelace

a rude twitch & we rudely straighten up… now where were we…

We pat down our rude feathers

in America

Mistaken identity

Sacramento. We were two feral cats passing on the stairs.

He wheezed his way up to the top floor.

Years of pumping gas had left his lungs

burnt. Older than me, maybe three years

or five. Maybe as old as thirty. I am surprised to learn

he has a wife. I don't know anyone who does & she is

a crown of brown cocktail waitress hair & lovely smile that rushes

ahead of her.

The gas jockey is interested in my 250 cc. He crouches & runs his

hands over

the chrome parts & I remember the droplet of sweat on his wife's pale

neck.

July. July. Jesus. *Sweet Jesus* as I learned to say from the gas jockey.

To escape the heat, I get up at 2am & go out for a ride

through a poor neighbourhood one block back

from the river, a stretch of road with a seam of cold air. I ride

through it nice & slow. I hit warm air, chop

down & turn the bike around to ride by the same

large wooden houses & porches & half-naked black

butterflies fanning themselves.

One night one of the large fleshy women

yells out 'hey white boy!'

I was amazed –

who was she yelling out to?

'They know they are white, but they must not know what they know.'

It is true. It is

but we don't like to say

it

in case it

sounds negative –

like a failing we cannot correct

Speaking for myself, I feel at times…

& deep in my marrow

Cofferdam

an insulating space between two bulkheads in a ship's decks

We are... *and abeam of...*

We are as we like. They were as we liked

them to be.

What will you admit about yourself?

I regret stealing the Bob Dylan cassette – totally unnecessary.

I had the money. I could have paid for it. I gave the cassette

to a girl who had offered me her apartment for

when she would be away visiting her parents

over Thanksgiving. She held the Bob Dylan cassette

in her hand. Her confused eyes rallied.

She said it was very kind of me. I beamed. Then – stupidly –

said I had stolen it (thinking it would add to its allure).

She still let me stay in her apartment.

She kept a bowl of little chocolate hearts wrapped

in silver foil. I ate one, then another. The remaining

chocolates I rearranged to conceal the damage, then in a moment of

utter

abandon I ate a third one, then, as the remaining ones

looked a bit under-represented, I ate them too. I did leave

her a note to say I had eaten *all* the chocolates. I thought honesty

might restore me to her good books. It didn't occur

to me to replace the chocolates.

Vanity

in the gilt mirror behind the Highbury bar

an under-nourished face nods

as if it knows a thing or two

about civil war – my lips

still burnt from her last kiss –

and mercenary talk

of necklacing and the many virtues

of a machete

I nod   back at that gilt-edge reflection

to let the mercenary know

nothing can shock me   no amount of spoilt blood   no burning plane

so long as my burnt lips recall –

a light blue coat   she had started to

wear that Spring & which I liked   the clip of dark hair at her nape

her quick heels beneath the streetlights   the hitch of her shoulders

the heels   then just the coat, then that too   vanished.

Borderlands

into the boot of a car I am bundled, then driven

along a winding coastal road. It is night-time

when we stop, I hear crashing surf, then

smell dope. An hour passes – perhaps longer –

then the doors crack

open, and I brace myself.

Thinking,

how silly. How appalling and silly. I didn't think it would end

this way. How might I have avoided it?

The boot lifts and the stars rush

down. One of the kidnappers shouts *vamos*; and I do;

through sand dunes and shoreline

back to where I began the evening by asking strangers, in

a roundabout fashion, where am I?

In free fall

Baldy Mountain, Phoenix, Sacramento, Davis, Oakland, Little Rock,
Denver, LA, San Francisco, North Beach.
Outside Eugene, I woke to shouting. The woman in the seat next
to me nudged, and said, 'Hon, that girl down the back? She's gone
stabbed him, with a pair of scissors.'
At the next stop the boyfriend limped down the aisle looking oddly
pleased with himself – relieved to be invalided home from the war.
Outside the bus the tearful girlfriend fell into the arms of the waiting
cops,

> unstuck from its world
>
> a limpet has nothing left
>
> but providence. Chance

And off we went, back on to the freeway, into the night of truck lights
and billboards.

Local Beauties

Three years later

home again

on a bus in Petone awash

in a Soviet hour

on a Soviet bus & all the women in Soviet dresses smiling

 through the hard rubble of their daily agonies &

light dazzling gorse over the eastern hills into gold &

the oil storage tanks modest & practical

turned perfectly round & white

as they never were before I left

5 Studies of my father

on crutches

stooped over his stomach to do up a shoelace.

his calloused hands

I never saw swim.

in his coffin

death shock in him, grey eyes angry, interrupted

halfway through a coughing fit.

interiority

a desert island, a solitary palm tree.

study for a crucifixion

his hands tied to the steering wheel as he drives

down a road that will not let go of him.

Traffic

In north-facing hospital windows

a burnt blue sky too beautiful

to speak over the top of.

A windowsill pigeon on parade.

We wonder what to ask the doctor –

his grim news drifts down to the street below

where traffic accelerates away from the lights.

On the facing wall a picture of a waterfall.

On the bedside table – flowers, an unread paperback.

On the overhead screen an Alaskan cruise ship sails by

her teeth and pink gums in a glass of water,

her fleshless slippers on the shiny floor.

We tiptoe away – catch the doctor once more –

filling his teacup on our way out.

Museum

We arrange the dead to look more dead.

We hoist up the dead cow & set its parchment & eye on an animal

lean, then place it in a dead native tree &

twist its head about to make its jaws look set to bite the sky.

We provide a citation: *This animal once sipped at a creek, once sired,*

loved in its animal way.

We roll the head of an ox over, pull a blanket of earth up to its neck.

We tack up the old maps & forgotten stock routes over

photos of defrocked hills.

Two camels harnessed to an overturned carriage wait to be told their

passengers are dead & their world is over.

We were sailing confidently

Stitch of sea and sky, dependable as ever. In that direction we
sped. That is how it was. Then it all stopped.

II

We were like birds caught in a mist net.

III

I lived off memories, of a hill, people in the distance. The wonder of
it all. Like a field blooming with blue bells. An empty bus pulls into
the bus stop, in imitation of how life used to be, the driver waits at
the ticking traffic lights – their sound usually buried underfoot, the
traffic din, and electronic beeps. But the street that runs the length of
the city's golden mile is deserted. Shop windows all carry the same
message –
'Dear valued customer as per government announcement to tackle
Covid 19… please self-isolate…Dear friends we are going to miss you
as we hibernate… no cash or stock on premises. *Kia kaha*'

Log

Limp sails. Limp faces. Old jokes doing the rounds for the fifth time. The moans and groans about this and that – the most shocking things no longer shock. The smells. The verities of the human body – lesions, bites, running sores, nits, lice. Efforts made to give others space. The endless wait for a wind shift.

Abandoned city

a graveyard / silence

emphatic / as stone

city towers / like the ruins

of tomorrow.

a kaka was seen / flying

along the golden mile

of the Capital.

Misplaced things

    for a split second   something only I am supposed

to see

        I hear

    out of a red heart   turned black

a melody   a split second later   I cannot remember

in the parted air where I had *felt my passing*

Scruples

I don't like to touch dead birds – this is something that is well-known about me.

I don't like to see a bird flattened wing tip to wing tip & its beak burst against the road.

The decommissioning of the old grandstand

Through the turnstile by runs of rust

we file & climb up winter's still breath

to red-stickered Row Y

and a stagnant view

of drought-shattered trees clutching at

fragments –

a rotten smell

from white skin

where water used to run.

We were herded here by tribal elders –

shoved into rough knowledge.

How quick

we were to recognise a bad decision

but missed all the critical ones –

fair play and sewer outfalls –

a broken fence

simmering grass

a lone *puriri*

on a windswept hill of animal hide.

Shadows wobble on cracked plinths.

How could we, in our short pants,
have led cattle along the 'green
lanes,' calling out their pretty names.

For a while, drunks with nowhere to go
sat frozen on plastic seats, their feet rested
on a glassy roll of decanted spirits.

A hillside was shaken
out, the view unbolted, seats
dismantled – I managed to buy from Row Y
our old seats for a song, turned them into book
shelves for my fantasies, their black numbers
holding on to flakes of green peeling paint.

Junior geography

A junior geography of slide and territory

A feared house I walked quickly to get past

A meteorite we rushed outside to see – slip by

our unremarkable selves

A fish I landed on the wharf,

flapped madly, managed eye

contact just once.

People like us. I don't even know what

that refers to anymore.

High Anxiety

For an unbroken hour I watched on television the Ascension Council ceremonially transfer the duties of the crown to Charles. A room filled with men in white shirts and black ties. In the front row a line of solemn former prime ministers, a dishevelled Boris who gave the impression of an imperfectly folded up tent. I flicked back to Sky sports, ran through golf, car racing, NRL, paused at a rural rugby match watched by a cow, then returned to the palace. They were still there, standing, disgruntledly, a few now speaking to their neighbour, some (Cameron) giving the impression of listening. One whose teeth lit up (Blair) as if he had just sighted the cheese board. A handsome blonde woman in black, born to perform this one role in her life read out a proclamation. Prince William came forward to sign a document. Various others did the same. The handsome woman was last to sign. Their duty done they filed out the room, fondling their black ties.

Non-organic rubbish collection

On the lane down to the sea

bike frames in a tangle

worn tires & squeezed out intestines

a sky dish & satellites of mould

A birdcage, its door left open

A sodden couch where three generations of women sat

twisting their hair while listening to Leonard Cohen

The mattress put out by the people three houses down stained

with sweat & marital discord

Old maps pulled out of shape by lust

Fox hunting scenes, anniversary cake tins, manual typewriters (God

bless their souls)

Leather-strapped suitcases, border stickered, Gambia, Tibet,

Madagascar

Holiday snaps of road trips to places whose names have since lapsed,

in model cars that no longer exist.

Bonfire

We smiled perhaps too hard,

as we fed the flames.

The crackling, it did sound

wonderful,

and around cold shadows

our smiles blew bright.

I tossed in an old

wooden sword – from when I was a

knight playing at virtue and valour,

it burned without a gasp.

We went on burning a hole in the night,

scrounging round to find more to

feed any tremoring ember.

Until the timid flames seemed to ask,

Are you sure? Are you sure?

At the change of tide

dismembered

in soft sand

a toothy clasp of

pointless appetite

ends

in a spine

picked clean

of flesh

elsewhere, homes

blown apart

white roofs pitch up

ransacked

a pincered arm floats away on the tide

the rest is left to rot

the frenzied

savage

pull of flesh

gnawed and

dragged

and gobbled up

medieval, carefree

bones, strewn

devourers defecate

the devoured

flesh and spirit

signposting

sites of mutilation

across a neighbourhood

powerless

to prevent or stop

such openness

no waste

of moral spent

no wishy washy horse shit

sung from a pulpit for those devoured &

shat out

just the facts

of life

death

crunching

underfoot

oh, what a beautiful day, the sun is out

The new neighbourhood

You blunder/ into places / you have not been invited

a shook branch / settles

is this the right place?

noon / quiet / dense / pencil lead / siesta

you gaze up / at a ceiling fresco / of birds in flight

is it dead / or alive / where one steps through / what shapes

the day?

Interview with great granddaughter from the future

Your boat crashed ashore, right?

Shipwrecked, yes. The steering pin snapped, the boat foundered.

Eventually I washed ashore, not far from White's Hotel.

So you knew where you were?

It was a bit later... after I got up for a look around, I thought it very

much resembled where I had just set out from...

Home?

The fade of somewhere already passed through. Yes. The close huddle

of hills, pitched rooves, the hydrangeas. I made my way to Whites.

A hotel known to you?

No. But I recognised everything about it. White in every direction. It

was a bit like being in endless agreement with yourself. The picture of

Cook's *Endeavour* on the wall a puzzle – until it wasn't.

Were you happy there?

I had a functioning toilet. A toilet seat, a working flush. Cook's men

squatted over a hole in a plank cantilevered over the waves, used a

frayed rope with a tasselled end to wipe their arses, dipping it into

the sea after.

I had a handy window through which the day passed its gifts.

I am reluctant to complain.

We have a transcript of a conversation where you are referred to.

Would you like me to read it back to you?

Pause.

If it is not too painful.

How old is he?

Sixty. Maybe older. I don't know.

By himself? You did say a bloke.

Yes, he gave the name Herodotus. He's a writer. I think he said...

Pause

Clean?

He has been traveling.

From where?

Well, he said... He said he'd been travelling in a dark wood.

Yes, yes. Does he understand what is required, the demands of the job.

He said he is a night owl. He doesn't sleep. The word he used is insomniac.

Pause

You explained the arrangement?

Full board in exchange for night clerk duties.

And he is ok with it?

Yes.

And he understands the responsibility. He will be in full charge of between the hours 10pm until dawn? He understands what that involves?

Yes. Yes. I explained …He is more than happy. He is not after a career in hospitality. As I said, he is a writer.

How did he strike you?

Quiet. Polite. He came through the interview well. Answered all the questions well, not a word more than required.

What kind of writer did he say he is?

I asked him that same question. He replied that he wrote lines.

As in sentences I suppose he means...

I asked that too, and he said he was happy to show me some samples. I did not accept the offer, as I felt my trust was under examination.

You didn't say if he had any special requests. They usually do you know.

He said he would need a desk and a chair, and the desk should be by a window. Also, he requested a room on the top floor.

There are only two floors.

I explained that too. Had I not been able to reassure him on that last point my impression is he would have terminated our interview.

What do you make of that?

I have no complaint.

You enjoy sailing...

I find it exhilarating.

Your Logbook puts it differently. I quote: 'I wonder if I haven't

adapted – or adapted fast enough?

Oh that. Yes. That reads true.

Adapt to what?

Wind shifts, new views. The eros of discovery... what a hotel room

arouses. You bound in the door... to a room you have never seen

before, made-up, new. You are likely to feel anything is possible.

My room at White's

The first time I flew against the window like an uncaged bird.

Across its walls I scratched my claws and felt a beaded pattern.

Three paces back and the idea of anything else beneath the coat of

white vanished.

A thick acrylic white in the bathroom shone with unpleasant

thoroughness.

The carpet, worn through, a crazy weave of shooting stars and

distress flares.

Otherwise, a white ceremonial air.

A serviceable white paint covered the door, inadvertent scuff

marks left in a guest's haste, the toe end of a shoe or a large, wrestled

suitcase.

A white bedspread, a ribbed texture, I named on the spot – the Bay of

Many Dunes.

Day one

I said good night to windows and woke to mirrors.

I got up, crossed the room for a look outside.

A vast crowd gathered beneath my window waved. Puzzling at first, but then, frankly, delightful.

Day two

I roll myself off the Bay of Many Dunes, stand, pat my stomach – cross the carpet.

The mirror swings open like a window. I lean out – to thousands of adoring faces.

They roar with approval; how natural it feels. Cannons are fired. The smoke clears. In the crowd I sense a wish for me to say something. I begin – with a homily that has since grown, and grows by the day, a recollection of my days where every wish of mine was met efficiently, without expectation of praise or reward. It is, or was, how shall I put, simply the way things are.

I am a guest – and you, dear reader, perhaps you are not.

You will wonder why you have been left outside, so to speak, and therefore why I was granted entry. You are surprised. Whereas for me there is no surprise, or if there is, it is surprise that you, reader, are surprised, even offended. Yes, I see the grievance in your face. You wish to blame. Perhaps I would feel the same way. Perhaps, when probably I mean, I would.

Look at the dotterels

Look at the dotterels

Their entire bodies distort

into instruments

that know only one note.

You stand back & wonder -

what it takes

to make just that one note &

to what ends?

They twitter & parade,

cackling like crazed aunts.

Log

On the windowsill, a small circling insect

in a saucer of gritty water. It tiny legs paw

a slow fruitless course.

How Cook must have dreaded days like this, the ocean

turned into a mirror to collect

long faces hanging over the ship's sides.

A few degrees south of the Tropic of Capricorn,

bagpipes rattling the still airs with *Lochaber No More.*

Fireworks in the background. Bastille Day celebrations on CNN.

Guests? They have disappeared like ants into the earth's cracks.

Log

A sunny afternoon, a ghostly haze in the lobby

as though a crowd smoking cigarettes

just wandered through

from the nineteen fifties.

Dusk, hard insistent white,

at last, the weatherboards

sink into night.

White is so pervasive,

it is hard to know where to start,

without risking a criticism as big

as the hotel itself.

We go about breakfast in silence – the wall portraits
unsettle. It is like being around English
people, a solitary and profoundly unhappy experience
of crunched toast, resolute privacy, and a smell of egg.

Log

At breakfast, a guest looked up from his egg to a neutral place, his
eyes soft and lost.

'Strange where she left the letter...Did I tell you?'

'On top of a tray of a dozen eggs...'

'...free-range ...'

A hoarded grief flooded his face.

It has been announced

New ground is to be broken over old ground.

New seasons are underway.

The wishing well

Gannets drop from the sky

Bright flashes dissolve in water

A girl runs out of a basement

In Kharkiv, rubble, a brave flower

There's a war on. There is always a war on.

Look at the windfall of

kanuka and manuka.

Wind is unfiltered, infantile.

It has no conscience.

A broken doll is powerless to ask why.

Often, I am in the Hague.

Usually in the shower and after

I've soaped, when

I am at my most enraged

but it always ends the same way.

I am just a naked white guy air-drying in a

shower box,

like the preening leaves

on the track down to Whakanewha

ready at last to speak –

soon the sky gives up and moves on.

There is a war on. There is always a war on.

Resumption of interview with great granddaughter from the future

May I ask if you are a patriot?

To what?

This country.

And which country is that?

The one you live in.

Where I live is a very small part of it. I can speak only of the room

where I sit at my desk and do my work. I have memories but the place

of memory no longer exists or is fast fading. So where would you

have me hoist my flag?

In *Cook's Journal* the coastline peters out… That unchartered space

is where I choose to dwell. I am, as you can see, prejudicially yours, a

cork bobbing in your opinion, for anger to aim a stone at.

We circle the pound with our heads down.

We stop to do up a shoelace.

We are supposed to be in an art class.

We are afraid to lift a brush in case

the paint betrays us.

You need to fix your tongue. It is not quite properly set in your mouth.

A little twist the other way, that's it.

pause

You helped dispose of heirlooms...

Yes. It was after the grandstand was dismantled and the old views decommissioned. We took down the pictures and drove them to the dump – the whiskered faces, bonneted women, the tumble weed of children – all of it had to go.

We made a large pile on the beach. It took all afternoon. On my last trip to the beach, I felt a new quickness. A rush to the side of expedience. Someone else poured on the kerosene. I threw on a match. A fumy air turned into a blue green shimmer, then a crackling flame tore across a man's striped pyjama top, and that was the past spoken for.

You sound sympathetic?

Imagine, if you will, a child with its head twisted round to face an unyielding past.

pause

You did say, 'burn the hotel down and start again.' It's in your Log.

I'd drunk too much. I was in an extravagant mood...

To destroy the hotel?

To shift it on to new foundations.

Memory is in the room next door

& still/ her head is turned from your bitter news / at leaving for
brighter birdsong / more colourful feathers
you walk around this bitter memory / and you cry – this is the wrong
room. *Take me to my room.*
you cry in vain/for another room/ a better room/ one that remembers
better.
the door flies open / old life spills towards you / a kitchen sink piled
high with unwashed dishes / a roasted duck / two manuka stakes / a
sagging wire pegged with washing / old dogs / quivering hinds / half
appetite / half supplication / the girl / at the bus stop / still she waits/
she was there yesterday / oh, that's right/ you'd forgotten /that's
right / that's right/ Federer & Nadal were in a fifth set / it all comes
back / the relief it was over / all that tension / unbearable / the sight
of Federer courtside / inconsolable / his head buried under a towel
/ like the way the French President chose to die / eating a humming
bird in a marinade of brandy / a towel over his head to hide his
appetite / to hide his shame.

the blue bike/the new paint / the blood smell of excitement/ matted
dog fur/the dog long gone / under a car wheel/ transgressions/
confusing terms / *chaperone*/alerting you to / skirt / thigh blushes
/ the word *hosiery* / the sad grammar of all women your mother's

age / the word *courtesan* /useless / like an analogue phone / on-line

You Tube *resurrections*- the atom bomb falls/ and falls again / from

the ends of the earth Gareth Edwards finishes off the Barbarians

try / JFK is shot / again and again/ again the bomb falls / and now

Martin Luther King is shot / again / now it is Robert Kennedy's turn /

on re-play / Neil Armstrong bounces across the moon / a new virus

/ fascists march / the unbelievable / the unthinkable / it happens

again / and again/ a raised arm / lifting the rug on what was thought

to have been flushed down the drain / *I can't breathe* translated

into all the world's languages / typewriters warehoused / apologies

warehoused / genius outsourced to AI lookalikes / Van Gogh's

sunflowers bloom again/ a robot named 'Rita' sings like Maria Callas

/ the offspring of the legendary lover sue the manufacturer of a new

sex toy branded Casanova / said to outlast human passion / to the last

breath / brains outsourced to 'likes'/ an *Insta* poet praised the world

over for acting her age / it is said *she feels* / old emotion / there is

nothing new / say the grandmothers on the park benches / youth was

their story too.

they / float / like dust motes / old lovers / coats / dresses / trousers /

scratchy jeans / sweatpants / underwear / bras / gathered / to catch

vanished flesh / piled shoes / shrunken for want of a foot / lives
shedding / as they tear through the century.

Log

At breakfast, the hotelier looked tired. The big toe
of him sticking out the end of his dressing gown like some faded
arrangement of gentry fallen on hard times.
It is exhausting to go from one crisis to another.
Light winds. Leaves scattering across the square.
A feeling of doors opening somewhere, and indoor faces blinking
back at sunshine.
The roof cracked at mid-day, the first time for months.

Tourist

I watched on TV

a spider

cast a silk loom net

all four corners of it

onto a cricket.

I watched – the cricket's tiresome effort

 to free its sticky limbs – and the spider's

first deliberate steps along a silk rope

to its prey.

I wondered, who am I?

The spider, or the cricket?

And how is it I know what is about to happen?

A question that is also an answer.

The threat at mid-tide

> sulphurous air &
>
> mud breath &
>
> claw marks left
>
> by feathered boxes
>
> prospecting on
>
> stilts

A circled eye pops
it hurries away on
thin twitching legs
head over breast
to warn others.

You yell / through cupped hands / *I am not your enemy. I am not your enemy.*

The feathered ball stops,
turns its head.

Once in a city park in America a

female jogger leashed to a dog reared

up at the sight of you and

pulling on the leash diverted

onto another path.

The others lift a wing,

shuffle closer to one another.

They chatter about you,

not to you.

They fan out.

They look back

over hunched shoulders.

You are not unwelcome /

just

not welcome.

Log

"And I only am escaped alone to tell thee"...a line Melville lifted from
Job.

Celerity. Melville's term for swift response.

But I shuffle like an old coal hulk pulling on its chains.

Across the mudflats, pools invent

stilts to balance in.

Reflected purpose

everywhere I look.

Now someone else is in the red telephone box

their hands pressed against the bleary

glass

  gently insisting you

                    climb down &

start again if you dare   *& return to*

the old neighbourhood   *to grow all over again*

The birds of Whakanewha

You walk on
with a half-wit's smile
through a neighbourhood with all its
curtains closed

where locals sit in
silent self-regard
a line of black berets on a
wooden bench in rural France

preening –

a blind eye turned to the village
idiot rolling in dirt to get
lice out of its feathers,
a strange custom that may pass
to you
in time.

They sleep as we do.
They wait or appear to.

They peer as you do

at the outgoing tide.

They store in their feathered

breasts

secrets & taboo items

a red fungal material &

a portion of flesh with an eye

to watch itself be eaten.

Accept without judgement their fossick through broken homes

Remember Napoleon's *armée* carried off from Moscow silken

petticoats, family heirlooms, a child's toy for their own.

Think of the penguin who after many weeks away must regurgitate

the contents of its stomach into the searching beaks of its young.

A fish jumps – for a split-second a world for which it has no name –

comes into view.

The flesh of a periwinkle can lead a local to smell and taste a home

they will never enter.

In the world of silhouettes

A wooden footbridge

conveys you away

from the breeding area like

in the old days when curtains

were drawn and you

were sent out to the back –

yard, to idle and ponder

the word 'rest'

as you do the word 'detour'

posted in front of the sacking

and hearing again the snip

on the bedroom door, as

you waited and watched

the back window for

the curtain to shift and

signal to come back inside.

New coordinates

the way down is a whole new direction / hold up your hands /step /

see how the fog sinks / and the nikau rise /

ringed with composure / down / to crumbling litter /

from yesteryear.

On the track down to Whakanewha / forgive /

the kererū its clumsiness / there is no right /

way to break out of a bad dream.

Log

A lousy sleep. A reel of dream running over it.

White cliffs – danger, danger –

The night desk

So much time is lost

looking up from *Moby Dick* to check if the moth on

the ceiling has moved.

Tea and toast at 3am

Last night I rang an old girlfriend in Germany. I could hardly hear

her. I had to shout, 'Why are you whispering?'

3am is the loneliest hour for –

cakeshops

glass fruit bowls and

stuffed toys

and listening to country music.

4am I return to the index of *Moby Dick*.

Simon, a Syrian monk, spent the last thirty-seven years of

his life on top of a pillar.

In the Kaikoura earthquake, the land dropped, then split – a cow

was left standing on a tiny island of land, its great head

lowered to the abyss beneath its feet.

Simon the monk was a *stylite!* The cow was just a cow.

6am. I doze off.

If I close my eyes, I see myself

effortlessly

as a pool of water

drawing

reflection.

6.31am. Compile a list of irritations:

What do the masses look like? What do the masses wear? What do white people think? What do black people think…? Presumptions – literature doesn't have much to say about, as character can only flesh out one person at a time.

7am. Begin personal essay on the contradictions of self-awareness.

7.15am. Stare far too long at a picture on the lobby wall of cattle standing in the tide, shitting on their reflections.

Blackbird

Look at that

blackbird. Beak

Up. Stomach, forgotten.

Look. It is flying.

Look at the other blackbirds.

Look at the sky. The sky is filled.

How did that happen?

The sky is a blackbird.

compass

yellow   flower bud, perfect scale.

dinner plate   cupboard grime, bitter evenings.

orange

rug   cigarette burn   fervent   a wish for it to disappear.

lava lamp   glow   beware.

Blue

Shoes   that sing.

ink   brush   strokes of grace.

bird   sonic notes   the sky composes.

Today I have decided to switch to *laughter* –

Anything at all

But a war is on – several wars in fact.

I did see something funny.

A dog with floppy ears walking along unaware a war was on.

At the railway station I bought a chocolate bar

and bit into it with old greed.

Dawn

I can tell by the dog bird sound

& crunch underfoot

& by the sun strike in the branches

& the broken sea in the bright green leaves.

I turn left which means the shorter walk -

the one that drags first light over my shoulder.

It is always like this.

Yet this morning is *this* morning

& I wonder

should I find room for the coughing fit heard from below the road?

Or the waves rattling ashore sou westerly by name -

I mean, are they relevant?

What about the fat kererū a feathered Buddha swaying on a branch?

Then I worry about making stuff up, i.e. the feathered Buddha

It is morning.

What's wrong with saying that?

Or here *I am*. I am up. I am in it.

Why must the nikau pod remind me of a sagging stomach

on a border official in the old GDR?

Why this mental rush to place the nikau in GDR uniform?

What is wrong with – here are the nikau or here I am, passing the

nikau?

I once had a night job counting people in & out of a computer facility. So what? I don't know what / I was twenty-two / now I am sixty-odd / something about that night job the nikau do not want me to forget. Across the water/ a growling car on Gordon's Road / a note from a tui's broken voice box & I remember a Chinese opera diva's song / about a cat with a chicken in its mouth.

What is wrong with simply saying I heard a car on Gordon's Road and a tui's song?

A mosquito buzzes near my ear. I want to say buzzes officiously. I want to say GDR.

I move on / making up the day.

To bring to

to counter-act

the daily battle

between what is there in front

of me, and random thought running to

serpents, and old maps.

The news of the day

After the boom of a passing aeroplane

I am showered by twigs.

It is a blowy day, and I am on a walk.

Ideally that is when things should happen.

Things are happening –

I was walking – now I am resting

on a mat of sun-dried reeds

above a swollen brown river.

I wanted the bench in the sun but a young woman

got to it first.

You see, things are happening –

I was anticipated.

Now she gets up and I sit where she

sat.

A lot is going on.

The river I have mentioned,

but not the dead bodies floating by –

toes pointed up, mouths shaped to O dear O dear

But that is a different river back in another life.

That is how it is.

The day is unstable

with so many things saying over and over to me –

You are *here*

You are *here*

In fact, I am all over the place.

And yet I never deviate from the path.

It is the same walk I do each day.

Last night I watched on TV the hearings

into UFOs in Washington.

A woman who said she had been abducted by aliens

sat very smugly looking back at

the world on all its couches.

I wonder what kind of walk would be

enough for her.

I haven't even got to the blue sky,

or – wow! – the green shoots of spring.

Yesterday a large woman burst into the lobby, and

cried, the daffodils are out! – and we all spun round to look.

I ate an ice cream – coconut and stracciatella –

a highlight I wish never ended.

I've also started using a pencil again –

I had completely forgotten the fun of a pencil sharpener.

I sharpened a pencil then swept up the shavings and fed them to the flames in the pot belly, then sat to watch

the offcuts of my failed words burning bright.

Neighbourhood watch

at a dark hour

comes the rubbish truck

in prowling gear –

a quick acceleration, a small triumph –

& on it goes, up & up the street &

down the laneway at the back.

It is the unseen work

that grips the eye.

It is just on light when I see

the woman at loose attention

outside the brick church,

head bowed,

a long silver ponytail

over her shoulders to the waist

of her track pants.

A minute later I would

have missed her

as she turned & jogged

past the upturned rubbish bins.

Herodotus in winter

By an old wooden fence knuckled

with spray painted graffiti

a woman in a blue coat

enters the bricked kiln of prayer.

The dead bird I saw yesterday

is still dead today.

On the train

platform

icy breath of

commuters struck

by quick sunlight.

The slow thought, the slow cold.

I slow walk, insistent,

as a wave –

frozen mid-

leap, and

puzzled –

by the blue-timbered chapel

at the edge of the ice.

In Antarctica I also saw a Sufi

mirage, Manhattan, dark, levitated –

the sun pushing through the murk

of a freight plane skidding to a halt.

It is my sixty-eighth winter.

In the children's tale everyone turns into stone.

I must deadhead the old lavender.

Whakanewha

Through a dead forest we walk down to meet the tide –

this wet coat fish put on

to meet their ancestral kin

 on curdled sand –

a burial chamber for creatures run out of air –

greeted by withered palms.

The tide is in.

Perhaps this is all I meant to say.

Then I remembered you and me at its edge

reeling in our shadows.

It was in the past this future too.

in sleep I return to the grove of the forest

In sleep I return to the grove of the forest
where insects plunder old newspaper headlines

& a gannet crashes into the sea beneath the cliffs
& a man with no limbs pushes himself along on a wheeled plank.

Oranges are for sale in a century not my own.
An army in bandages is in retreat, ice, blood, frozen horses.

In sleep I return to the old newspaper headlines,
to a century not my own when oranges were for sale.

A man with no limbs watches a gannet crash into the sea
& pushes his plank beneath the cliffs.

In sleep I return to the plundered forest,
to the grove of a century not my own.

Across the harbour in April

city lights stray   deaf   to the night sea

last winter's lover   walks   hand in hand   with another

mid-tide   two shags   spread their black wings   a ship passed

acknowledgements

On page 33, the title of the poem 'They know they are white, but they must not know what they know' is a line from a Claudine Rankine poem.

Rankine goes on to instructively write, 'The writer's essential strangeness is his greatest resource. To be in sceptical tension with our own inclinations… because those inclinations are partly an inheritance for a racial imagining that both is and is not his.'

The title of the poem, 'I'm waving to can't see me anymore' on page 27 a phrase from a line of Rankine's poem, Similarly, my sister.' '…like the wave until I realise the ones I'm waving to can't see me anymore.'

The Southern Review, Baton Rouge, Vol 32, issue 3, July, 1996.

On page 62 the phrase 'a dark wood' is from Dante's *Divine Comedy*.

I would like to thank friends and colleagues who gave encouraging feedback to this book when it was still in manuscript form. In particular I owe a debt of gratitude to Ian Wedde, and to James Brown for his helpful and wise comments, and to Felicity Plunkett for lending her own fine eye for concision to my lines. And lastly to Terri-ann White, for the guiding inspiration behind the Upswell poetry series.

About Upswell

Upswell Publishing was established in
2021 by Terri-ann White as a not-for-profit
press. A perceived gap in the market for
distinctive literary works in fiction, poetry
and narrative non-fiction was the motivation.
In her years as a bookseller, writer and then
publisher, Terri-ann has maintained a watch
on literary books and the way they insinuate
themselves into a cultural space and are
then located within our literary and cultural
inheritance. She is interested in making books
to last: books with the potential to still be
noticed, and noted, after decades and thus
be ripe to influence new literary histories.

About this typeface

Book designer Becky Chilcott chose
Foundry Origin not only as a strong,
carefully considered, and dependable
typeface, but also to honour her late
friend and mentor, type designer Freda
Sack, who oversaw the project. Designed
by Freda's long-standing colleague,
Stuart de Rozario, much like Upswell
Publishing, Foundry Origin was created
out of the desire to say something new.